This new series, published by Medio Media/Arthur James, responds to the spiritual needs of people living today's busy and stressed lifestyle. Each book in the series is designed to allow the reader to develop a space for silence and solitude and spiritual practice in the context of ordinary life or by taking a short period of withdrawal. The structure of the book allows a flexible time-table to be constructed which integrates periods of reading, physical practice or exercise, and meditation.

Fr Charles A. E. Brandt lives as a hermit monk on the Oyster River on Vancouver Island. He was ordained to the priesthood by Bishop Remi de Roo in Courtenay in 1967, with a mandate to live the hermit life. He is an oblate of Saccidananda Ashram (Camaldolese Benedictine), Tamil Nadu, India, one of whose founders was Dom Bede Griffiths.

He has been honoured for his environmental work with the Cal Woods Environmental Award and the Haig Brown Conservation Award. He has recently appeared on the CBC television shows *Man Alive* and *On the Road Again*.

Fr Charles earns his living as a professional book and paper conservator, recently completing the restoration of the Nurmburg Chronicles, printed in 1493. He teaches a course in Curatorial Care of Paper at the University of Victoria through the Fine Arts Department.

An ardent fly-fisherman and keen birder, Fr Charles holds a bachelor of Science degree from Cornell University and a Bachelor of Divinity degree from Nashotah House Seminary.

His childhood hero was Henry David Thoreau who 'took the woods to find what life was all about'. While studying ornithology at Cornell University he became acquainted with Starker Leopold, the son of Aldo Leopold, author of *Sand County Almanac* and the father of North American Ecology.

The 'On Retreat With ...' Series

SELF AND ENVIRONMENT

On Retreat With
Charles Brandt

MEDIO MEDIA/ARTHUR JAMES

LONDON AND BERKHAMSTED

First published in Great Britain in 1997 by

MEDIO MEDIA LTD
in association with
ARTHUR JAMES LTD
70 Cross Oak Road
Berkhamsted
Hertfordshire HP4 3HZ

© Charles A. E. Brandt 1997

Charles A. E. Brandt asserts the moral right
to be identified as the author of this work.

A catalogue record for this book is available
from the British Library.

ISBN 0 85305 427 4

Typeset in Monotype Bulmer by
Strathmore Publishing Services, London N7

Printed and bound in Great Britain by
Guernsey Press Ltd, Guernsey, C.I.

Contents

[5]

Being on retreat:
how to do it yourself

Stay in your cell and your cell will teach you everything.

– Saying of the Desert Fathers

The problems of the world arise from people's inability to sit still in their own room.

– Pascal, *Pensées*

Why set aside time for retreat?
Nature believes in retreats. Each day we virtually shut down our active processes of mind and body for the retreat and renewal we call sleep. Each year the animal and vegetable worlds go through periods of deep rest we call hibernation. These are not escapes from reality but ways of becoming more deeply attuned to reality, respecting its ways and trusting the inherent wisdom of nature.

Between each breath there is a moment of cessation, of deep stillness, which is not the stillness of inaction but the stillness of non-action. Between periods of daily work we naturally trust the mind and body when they tell us to rest. Between two thoughts there is an instant of mental silence.

On the London Underground, many stations have a recorded announcement each time the train stops, warning passengers stepping from the train to the platform to 'mind the gap'. Minding the gap is what this book is about – helping you, we hope, to see and respect the natural human need to retreat from action and speech at set times so that we can return to speech and action refreshed, re-balanced and renewed.

The spiritual life is not a specialized part of daily life. Everything you do in the day, from washing to eating breakfast, having meetings, driving to work, solving problems, making more problems for yourself once you have solved them, watching television or deciding instead to read, going to a restaurant or a movie or going to church, *everything* you do is your spiritual life. It is only a matter of how consciously you do these ordinary things, how attentive you are to the opportunities they offer for growth, for enjoyment, and how mindfully, how selflessly, how compassionately you perform them. Yet to live life spiritually all the time everyone needs to take specific times to focus on the spiritual dimension before everything else.

'Set your mind on God's kingdom and his justice before everything else, and all the rest will come to you as well.' Jesus said this in his Sermon on the Mount (Matt. 6:33). Taking a time of retreat will help you discover what he means by 'kingdom' and 'justice'. It will teach you that the kingdom is not a place but an experience of presence. The kingdom is within us and all around us. And you will learn that justice means balance, harmony, order. We hunger for justice in all the activities and relationships of our lives.

Buddhists see the spiritual significance of daily life in terms of ordinary mindfulness: doing everything with awareness, wakefulness. Christians similarly have long worked at praying at all times, giving glory to God in everything they do, practising the presence of God. This does not mean going around muttering prayers to yourself all day. You would only be more distracted in what you are doing. Nor does it mean thinking about God all the time. That would make you a religious fanatic. Praying ceaselessly, practising the divine presence is not something extra we do but the way we do whatever we are doing. It is a way of *being* in the midst of action: of being-in-action.

Perhaps the best comparison is with a relationship with someone you love. The awareness, the mindfulness, of that love surrounds and permeates you and all your words and responses all the day. You do not have to be thinking of the person you love all the time but they are with you and their often silent presence transforms your consciousness. Yet at the end of the day, or whenever opportunity allows, you return to the full presence of that person. Being with them helps the relationship to grow and deepen, even when romance wears thin. The 'quality times' together are essential for the health and development of love.

How to set up a retreat

The 'On Retreat With …' series has been prepared to help you to spend quality time in the most fundamental relationship of your life, your relationship with God. In the ground of this relationship are planted all your human relationships, even your relationship with yourself. Quality time with someone requires a certain degree of exclusivity – you say *no* to other invitations and pleasant opportunities in order to concentrate on your presence with one person. Other jobs and responsibilities go on hold. When you return to address them you will be refreshed, calmer, and you can see the problems that easily overwhelm you in a better perspective. Retreat is not escape. You make a retreat in order to address reality more realistically and courageously. Retreat does not solve your problems but it helps you deal with them in a more peaceful and hopeful way. This is the meaning of a retreat: we retreat in order to advance deeper into the mystery of love's reality.

This book can help you structure your time and set the tone for the period of retreat you are allowing yourself to take. As life today is very busy and as it often seems impossible to find time for silence, stillness, and non-action, we need all the help we can get in order to take the time of spiritual retreat which both spiritual and psycho-logical health require.

Time and place: your cell

You do not need to take a great stretch of time to make a retreat. But you need to designate a certain period of time and stick to it. It could be an hour, a morning or afternoon, a day, a weekend, a week, three months. In some traditions five-year retreats are customary. Let's start with a couple of hours.

If it is a short time, a couple of hours, you will probably be at home. Or you may have found you have some free time when away on holiday or a business trip. You do not have to fill in the empty space in the agenda: keep it empty. Go into the emptiness and you will emerge refreshed, more fulfilled. Set the time realistically. Put your answer-phone on. Turn the television or radio off. If you need to tell someone not to disturb you for the next couple of hours, do so. Put your work away or walk away from it. Then make a space.

The early Christian monks who lived much in solitude each had a cell. A monastic cell is different from a prison cell: you choose to be there. It is a place of stability, of security, of focus. It does not have to be elaborate. Cells are simple places. A chair, a cushion on the floor, a corner of a room. Make it tidy and clean. Set up a symbol of the presence; this could be a candle – ancient symbol of the presence of Christ – a flower, an icon, a photo, a cross, a

Bible, or a simple everyday object. There should be a sense of simplicity, not clutter – of beauty, not prettiness. Have a watch or clock with a timer device nearby (not a loud ticker or too prominently placed).

With steadiness and ease: your body
Your retreat is a homecoming, an integrating, a remembering. It is not a spacewalk or a mind trip. You cannot come home unless you come inside, so take time to consider that you are also taking time to *make friends with your body*. And remember that you are only singling out the body for the purpose of the retreat. In fact you are really one single-woven tapestry of body–mind soaked and grounded in spirit: one being, fully alive.

Single out the body, then, and learn that it is happy to carry you, support you, hug you. It rejoices to pump blood, breathe, digest, walk, and sleep. It is a wonderful, mystical, funny contraption in which we are incarnated, and have epiphanies and transfigurations, and are crucified and resurrected.

Whatever you do on this retreat, keep breathing. Breathe as you take breakfast, as you go for a solitary walk or do some housework in your cell. Breathe while you are on the toilet. Breathe during your spiritual reading and as you doze off to a peaceful sleep after your day of silence.

You already have the three things necessary with which to make friends with your body. They are breath, gravity, and ground. You have been breathing since you were born and you will keep doing so as long as you need to. So relax and let breath breathe you. It is closer to you than your thinking. The way you breathe determines how you feel (see how your breathing changes when you are angry, frightened, or peaceful). As you give your attention to your breath you become naturally heavy. That is gravity hugging you. Give to it. Let it take you to the ground which stands under you (*understands you*). The ground comes up to hold you, so relax and do nothing. In fact, un-do. Let it. You just pay attention to the breath as it breathes you in and out, in and out.

You might enjoy lying on your back before and/or after your meditation times, or after a walk. Lying on your back is an excellent way to start making friends with your body on this retreat. It helps turn off all the tapes playing in your head: tapes telling you to make a good impression on others, to be demure or macho, how to look sexy or respectable, how to dominate and be noticed. When you lie down, the three bony boxes of your body – the head, chest, and pelvis – stop chattering to each other for a while and relate directly to the ground instead. It is like turning gravity off for a moment.

Lie on your back with your knees bent so that your lower back is quite flat on the floor. Let your chin drop lightly towards your chest so that it is no longer pointing up to the ceiling. If this is difficult, put a folded blanket under your head, just an inch or so, no more. And stay, and wait in silence or listen to a taped talk on meditation or some music. If you doze off, so be it. When you do get up, first roll over gently on to your hands and knees. It is not helpful to yank the head straightaway in order to get up, because that immediately undoes all the work that breath, gravity, and ground have just accomplished in straightening you out and unknotting you.

If you want to take this friendship with your body further, you could read *Awakening the Spine* by Vanda Scaravelli, *Yoga Over 50* by Mary Stewart (even if you are 25), and *Yoga and You* by Esther Myers. These three women are yoga teachers of great depth, humour, and insight.

Lectio: your mind and its emotions

Then, sitting comfortably, read a section of this book. Read slowly. The book will last a long time, longer, probably, than your body. So there is no need to speed-read or devour the book and get on to another one. Re-read what you have read. Let your mind settle on a part of the passage which speaks to you most deeply. This may be just a phrase, a word, an image, or an idea. Revolve around that for a while. You don't have to analyse it. Savour it. The early desert monks called this *lectio*, spiritual (rather than mental) reading.

After a period of *lectio*, which can be ten or fifteen minutes, transfer your attention to the symbol which is the focal point for your retreat-space. Let your attention move towards the symbol, into the presence in the symbol. Let thought relax and the mind be still. When thoughts, fantasies, fears, anxieties, restlessness surface, let them come and let them go. Say, 'I'm sorry, you'll have to come and see me later. I'm busy doing nothing at the moment.' They will get the message if you give it strongly; be ruthless with them and don't compromise.

Meditation: going deeper

This would be a good time now for your meditation. Depending on how long you have been meditating or if you are just beginning, decide how many periods of meditation you are going to have during your retreat. A minimum would be two a day. Don't overdo it, but if you are a regular meditator you can profitably put additional periods in. More is not automatically better, of course. Three would be moderate. Six periods would be fine if you were sure you were not straining yourself or getting greedy.

Sit down with your back straight, sit still, close your eyes. Take a few deep breaths and then breathe normally. Then, silently, begin to repeat your word, your mantra. A good Christian mantra is the word *maranatha*. It means, 'Come, Lord,' or, 'The Lord comes,' but do not think of its meaning as you say it. Say the word simply and listen to it as you say it. This is the journey of faith, the deep listening. Faith leads to love. You could also take the word *Jesus* or *abba* (an Aramaic word used by Jesus, meaning 'father'). Whatever word you choose, stay with the same word throughout the meditation (and from one meditation period to the next) so that it can progressively take you deeper, from mind to heart.

Do not say the word with force. You are not trying to blank out the mind. Do not fight the thoughts which will come to you from every direction. Keep returning to the mantra. Say the word from the beginning to the end of the meditation whether you are aware of feeling distracted or peaceful. As soon as you realize you have stopped saying the word, start saying it again. In time (anywhere between five minutes and twenty years) the mantra will lead you at moments into complete stillness and silence, beyond itself. But if you are conscious of being silent then you are not yet completely silent, so keep on saying the mantra until the Spirit takes over. You will find that you say the mantra more deeply, more finely, more delicately as time goes on. Time your meditation with a timer – not too alarming a sound. If you are new to meditation, begin with twenty minutes (or less if you really find twenty too long). Otherwise thirty minutes is a good period to meditate for. If you have a gong, this will help lead into and out of the meditation peacefully.

After the meditation, come out slowly. Open your eyes. Pay attention to the symbol you have set up in front of you. This would be a good time to read some scripture. *The Burning Heart* would be a good book to use at this point – a collection of John Main's favourite Scripture passages with a short commentary by him. Again, read slowly, chewing and savouring the Word. Don't gulp it down. You could then listen to some music, do some yoga, draw, or paint.

Structuring your time of retreat
If you have to get back to work and daily life, take a few moments to appreciate the gift of present you have just enjoyed – let it go, be non-possessive. Read another section of this book, again slowly and savouring what appeals to you. Open yourself to the next thing you have to do and prepare to do it while keeping your mind and heart open to the presence you have just turned towards. Your prayerfulness continues into whatever you are now going to do. And you can share the fruits of peace and joy you have received with others, not by preaching, but in the way you relate to them. If you need to, pack up your retreat things reverently and get on with life.

If you have more time you can vary the elements of this retreat time. If you have a whole day, for example, you could schedule two, three, or four meditations. This will depend somewhat on your experience in meditation. Don't overdo it, and more does not mean better. If you are making the retreat with others, that will introduce another dimension of presence. Use this book together, reading it aloud. If you have a weekend or even longer you will need to schedule your time more carefully. Draw up a timetable but allow yourself to be flexible in keeping to it. Morning, midday, and evening are natural times for prayer – and before you go to bed. If you have a day or longer on retreat, do some manual work, even housecleaning, and get some exercise and fresh air. Walk in the garden or a park. Take this book with you and stop and read a section during your walk.

Don't just do something, sit there!
You might find the voice of conscience attacking you during your retreat. 'You are wasting your time,' it will say, or, 'You are being selfish.' You will think of all the practical, urgent, problematic things you could do. You will get an insight into a situation and want to dash off to implement it. Watch these restless thoughts and they will die down and return less frequently. This is why you will benefit from scheduling your time. It will fool your bush mind into thinking you are doing something productive. But your heart will teach you that you are not trying to produce or achieve anything. You are being. You are drinking deep, in the desert of modern life, of the waters of divine being. Your work and the people you live with, will all benefit from this time of retreat, so you are not being selfish. A gentle discipline in ordering your time of retreat – whether an hour or a day or a weekend – will help awaken a sense of inner freedom from anxiety, obsession, and fear. Enjoy it: find joy in it.

Laurence Freeman

Self and Environment

Father Charles A. E. Brandt

It is early morning with its quiet and coolness. I walk out the old logging road to Catherwood Road. Catherwood is my connector to the outside world. My hermitage is located deep in the temperate rain forest, on the Oyster River, British Columbia. The logging road along with other trails through the forest is where I practise walking meditation. I do not think of the road as leading anywhere. It is the road to nowhere, the path on which I journey and have been journeying for a lifetime. When I walk this road I have no destination, no timetable or estimated time of arrival. I simply place one foot in front of the other, let all my cares, anguish, angst, fears drop away. My breathing is in harmony with my pace, my pace is in harmony with the rhythm of the universe. And although this is the path of nowhere, in reality it is the way to everywhere, because it enables me to enter into communion with the whole community of beings, beings which are diverse, interiorized, and each in communion with every other being in the universe. I become present to the most distant star, and she to me, the 'complicated web of interdependent relationships'. Every atom of my being is present to every atom in the universe, and they to it.

We shall not cease from exploration
And the end of all our exploring
will be to arrive where we started
And know the place for the first time.
– T. S. Eliot, *Four Quartets*

Humanity is set on a path of exploration that will lead
to the realization of the oneness of the human community
and the earth community. When that begins to happen
and when it does happen we will truly know the place for
the first time. We live in a dualistic, dysfunctional society
that is intent on exploiting the natural world. We are in a
crash situation, living between hope and despair. We have
approached the bottom closely enough for us to begin to
realize that we have to change. We sense that if we do not
change, the human species could very well disappear.
There is an attraction force present today beckoning us
away from the pit of despair to the hope of a better world.
A transformational process has begun that is leading us
into a new age, the age of the earth. This transformation
begins with the human heart, in the core of our spirit. We
begin to detect a spring welling up in our heart. Perhaps
it is now only a trickle. But it will never run dry. Some-
times it runs more clearly and evenly. At other times it
seems to have gone completely underground. It is a life
force that needs to be purified so that it will flow continuously. It will lead to a transformation of our hearts and
minds that will enable us to realize the unity of all beings

and enable us to reach out with love to every creature in the universe.

*

In my teens I discovered Spinoza. At the time I was reading Thoreau, Emerson, Walt Whitman. But probably it was Spinoza who inspired me to believe that if I could get close enough to nature I would come close to ultimate reality as well. It was Henry David Thoreau who used to walk early in the morning and even late at night attempting to develop latent senses that we have lost track of. I always interpreted Spinoza's teaching as panentheism, not pantheism. But it led me to take long walks (I was an ardent birder) during which times I attempted to open my consciousness to everything about me. This was an attempt to commune with nature, to enter into communion with all beings.

It was my first attempt to get in touch with that mysterious wisdom that seemed to underlie all things. This affinity with the natural world led to my teaching natural history subjects at Osceola Boy Scout Camp deep in the Ozarks of Missouri. It was there that I first came to know a bit about the First Nations who had been the original inhabitants of the region, and where I was called to enter the honorary tribe of Mic-O-Say and to advance from Brave to Sachem. It was through Mic-O-Say that I came to have a deeper respect and love for the earth, and to respect more deeply the Spirit that fills the whole earth.

After an Air Force career (non-combatant) and after

taking a science degree in ornithology from Cornell University, I began to look more seriously at religion. Entering Nashotah House Episcopal Seminary in Wisconsin I completed a B.D. But my main interest it seemed was in the contemplative life, especially after reading Thomas Merton's *Seven Storey Mountain* in 1950. This led me to England as an Anglican deacon to explore the contemplative religious houses. I entered the Community of the Resurrection at Mirfield and was ordained by the Bishop of Wakefield to the Anglican priesthood. Realizing that this was not the milieu for contemplative living, I returned to the New England states to live as an Anglican hermit under the guidance of the Holy Cross Fathers on the Hudson River. During these years I had been reading the Church Fathers and was drawn more and more to the Catholic Church. But it was not until I had entered the Anglican Benedictine Community at Three Rivers, Michigan, that I was given the courage and grace to enter 'heaven's gate'.

As novices at Three Rivers we read only Catholic spiritual books (with the Catholic imprimatur) and said and sang a Latin office and mass. During the course of my time there someone asked me if I had heard of the new book by Dom Bede Griffiths called *The Golden String*. This book, which had been published in 1955, eventually came into my hands through a gift from a friend. The prologue commences with a quotation from William Blake:

> I give you the end of a golden string;
> Only wind it into a ball,
> It will lead you in at heaven's gate,
> Built in Jerusalem's wall.

The autobiography describes Bede's journey from Oxford, through his conversion to the Catholic Church and his entrance into the Benedictine Community at Prinknash, and ends with his preparation for his journey to India. The latter part of his autobiography is found in a second book, *Return to the Centre*, in which he describes his India adventure and the discovery of 'the other half of his soul', which was a balancing of the discursive and intuitive dimensions of his being.

*

Some ten years later, after entering the Catholic Church and having spent eight years as a simply professed Trappist monk, I was given permission to join the Hermits of St John the Baptist at Courtenay, Vancouver Island, British Columbia. Received by the hermits, I was ordained to the Catholic priesthood by Bishop Remi J. De Roo, Bishop of Victoria, B.C., with a mandate from him to live the hermit life.

Dom Bede Griffiths wrote to me on 2 January 1992:

> Thank you very much for sending me the report
> on your hermit life in the *Island Catholic News*.
> I think that it is important that it should have

public recognition in the Church. I trust that you find that the transformation continues, as Fr Berry puts it, into a sense of oneness with the earth community and the human community. I think that this is the path on which we are being set.

Sr Pascaline Coffe, OSB, a friend who had given me direction, encouraged me to make a trip to India and spend some time at Fr Bede's ashram, Saccidananda Ashram in Tamil Nadu.

*

I had for years been actively concerned and involved in the environmental movement, especially since entering the Catholic Church and becoming a hermit monk, living in the temperate rain forest on the banks of the Oyster River on Vancouver Island. Immersed in the beauty of earth, I had taken rather bold stands against several of the logging and mining companies that seemed bound to destroy all that I had come to the rain forest for. It was apparent to me that there must be some better way of changing the destructive practices of the giant corporations than lying in front of their heavy equipment, or pointing out to others through writing and speaking what was actually happening to our life support systems. I knew that not only was a transformation of consciousness necessary in my own self, but that what was necessary was a new vision of reality that would bring about this transformation throughout the planet.

Before I left Canada, I had been reading Hugo Lasalle's *Living in the New Consciousness,* and had made notes on his thoughts. One day after the noon meal at Annanda Ashram (where those who were staying for a longer time at Saccidananda Ashram took up their residence), I was showing these reflections to Francis and Joanna Macy who had arrived several days before. I recall that Joanna asked me if I were acquainted with Deep Ecology. This was a new bit of terminology for me and through some questioning I attempted to come to some understanding of Deep Ecology. This eventually led me to the discovery of the writings of Thomas Berry and Brian Swimme. I find it interesting that I had to go to the East to learn how to enter into communion and harmony with the earth community.

*

Twenty-five years ago I applied to the diocesan council of priests to attend an environmental conference in one of the prairie provinces. The answer came back to me that the environment was not one of the main concerns of the council. Just recently the churches have begun to look at the environmental destruction that is taking place and have begun to realize that there is reason to be concerned. People like Thomas Berry, who have been preaching Deep Ecology in the wilderness for years, are finally being taken seriously and listened to. He and Dr Brian Swimme are more and more being invited to speak to the whole range of society, including the churches. They are talking about

[27]

the 'New Story', the earth story, the universe story. They teach that unless we can come to appreciate and understand this story, which is also our story, the human community may not go into the future.

In the depth of our being we have a longing to know the earth and its plan, to know the universe, and ourselves in its deepest and truest form, and to know Ultimate Reality. Somehow we suspect that if we could only come to the discovery of our true self we would arrive as well at the true meaning of the earth and universe. Especially today we want to understand the earth and its plan because there is a deep lurking fear within us that the viability of the human species depends on a healthy relationship with the earth, that our destiny is tied in with her destiny, that somehow we have to free ourselves from an exploitative relationship and move into a loving communion with the earth and all of her creatures. We know that we cannot simply *intend* this new relationship to occur. It lies more in the field of attention than in the field of intention. We sense that we have to undergo a transformation, a transformation that will lead us into a new mode of religious consciousness, give us a new vision of reality. We long to be free from the tyranny of the ego, and to open ourselves at the point of our spirit to the Spirit that fills the whole universe. And we know that to undertake this transformation we must be willing to enter into a kind of death, a death to the tyrannical ego. But the one thing that we fear most is death. We hesitate to make the entry into this new sphere of consciousness, partly out of fear (because there is no guarantee that we will arrive), and partly because we do not know how to open ourselves to the splendour that we suspect is there.

*

Today we are greatly concerned about where we, the human community and the community of the natural world, are going. We think of them as two communities, but in reality they form a single sacred community. Until we can see this unity we will continue to be diminished humans, since to be ourselves we need to enter into communion with all other beings. As well, until we come to the realization that we form a single sacred community we will continue to exploit and diminish all other beings. And so, the earnest question of our time continues to be, where are we going? What is our true destiny?

It is clear that we stand at a turning point. We are on the verge, or already in the midst, of creating a new mode of religious consciousness, a mode of consciousness that gathers up all previous forms of consciousness and then goes beyond them. We are in the midst of a transformation that occurs only rarely, perhaps once in a thousand years. I speak of a transformation of consciousness. We are at a crossroads on our journey of exploration, between the old consciousness and a new mode of consciousness, a religious mode of consciousness. We look forward to a better world, a kinder world. The transformation that I speak of is already in orbit. It is occurring in our thinking, in the perception of ourselves, and especially in the perception of our environment.

The expression 'paradigm shift' might be used to express this change. Man, in his evolution, has travelled through various spheres of consciousness, developing from an archaic consciousness, through a magical, mythical consciousness to a rational consciousness. We are entering – in fact have already entered – what Hugo Lasalle calls a new integral consciousness. This latter stage might be called 'fourth dimensional consciousness'. This is described as a totally new experience of reality with a freedom from the bonds of space and time. To enter this sphere we will have to overcome conceptual time – not eliminate, but overcome it. We will be led to know the place for the first time. We enter this sphere on the one hand through a deeper appreciation and wonder of the universe, and on the other through the practice of meditation, a type of meditation that is non-objective, where we open our spirit in its depth to the ultimate Spirit, to That Which Is.

Unless we undergo the transformation that leads us into this new consciousness, our earth could suffer not only biocide but geocide as well. Our present crisis is a clear sign warning us of the need for this new orientation. Our imprisonment by clock time adds to our failure to see things clearly. But we are on the verge of a new stage in human/earth development. The labour has already begun. We are being born into new levels of thinking that will result in the freedom that will allow us to fulfil our destiny, to become love in human form, to embrace all earth creatures as our sisters and brothers, and indeed our most distant sister stars as well. It will lead us from exploitation to the understanding that all creatures are a community of subjects to be communed with.

Our new thinking will be mystical thinking and we will come to develop an appreciation for the teaching of the great mystics such as Meister Eckhart, St John of the Cross, and others. As well, we will come to appreciate more deeply the spiritual writers and teachers of our own time: Bede Griffiths, Thomas Merton, John Main, Thomas Keating, William Johnson, the Dalai Lama, Pascaline Coffe, Hugo Lasalle, Laurence Freeman, Simone Weil, Jean Vanier, and many others.

> In the eternal birth that occurs in the core and
> innermost regions of the soul, God covers the
> soul with light, whereby the light grows so great
> in the core of our being that it overflows into the
> faculties of the soul and into the outer person.
>
> – Meister Eckhart

And there are the teachers who help us understand the dream of the earth: Thomas Berry, Brian Swimme, Frijof Capra, Jean Gibser, Teilhard de Chardin.

*

In the distance, on my early morning walk on the old logging road every day, in the first light, a robin begins its canticle. The song is taken up by the Swainson's Thrush and then the finches, and finally, a solitary vireo. The forest suddenly becomes a celebratory event, exploding into song and motion and joyous exchange of the community of beings communicating and articulating themselves in a grand celebratory event. They speak the story of the universe from its primordial flaring forth – the galactic story, the earth story, the life story, and the human story – down to the end of the cenozoic period where we now find ourselves. Because it is terminal we are fearful. We do not know yet whether or not we are a viable species, whether we will make it or not, whether we will come to know the place for the first time.

*

There is a new story that is being told today, although in fact, of course, it is an old, old story. It is the universe story, the earth story. The story comes from science, from quantum physics. It is a story that Plato or Aristotle, Thomas Aquinas, Galileo, Isaac Newton would not have known. It is a cosmological story that is just dawning on our minds and imagination. As Brian Swimme describes it, 'this universe is a single multiform energetic unfolding of matter, mind, intelligence, and life'. The universe as a whole behaves more like a developing being. It is a single, multiform, sequential, celebratory event. And we are integral with the story. Indeed, it is our story as well as the universe story. This is the story we have to come to understand, the story which describes our true journey.

But we have not been paying attention to the story or

to our part in the story. If we could learn to pay attention we would be able to go into the future. The importance of being attentive inspired the thought of three of the most influential thinkers of modern times. Simone Weil thought that the most important quality we could acquire in our lifetime was what she described as 'selfless attention'. Fritz Schumacher came to the same conclusion and stressed the importance of 'learning to attend'. Alfred Whitehead spoke of the importance of the student paying attention to the leaf under the microscope, seeing what is there.

If only we could learn to pay attention and teach others to do the same, I think we could come to appreciate the story of the universe. We could learn to commune with nature and the natural world, realizing that the natural world is a community of subjects to be communed with, not a collection of objects to be used and exploited. We would be able to get in touch with our own inmost self, and this primarily through meditation – for meditation is simply learning to pay attention. And finally we would come to discover our true cultural roots, roots which go back to the primordial flaring forth from fifteen billion years ago, and not just rest in our present consumer culture.

We all naturally have a sense of the sacred. From this sense of the sacred we shape our lives, our norms of social behaviour, our disciplines, even our explanation of life and how we relate to others about us and to the wider world. To develop our sense of the sacred, it is imperative that we have a true cultural formation. Unfortunately, today the cultural formation that is being provided by our institutions is no longer offering proper and adequate guidance to our sense of the sacred. This primarily because the institutions which are providing our cultural formation are unaware of the universe story. Our culture ultimately flows from the earth, from the universe, from Ultimate Reality.

To know and understand the story we have to return to the source. Traditionally we do this through the study of Scripture or of philosophy texts. But philosophy and Scripture tell us of creation in terms used many centuries ago. We cannot neglect this earlier way of returning to the source, because it is important. But our consciousness has developed enormously even since neolithic times. Today we have a new way of understanding how things emerged in the beginning and the sequential transformations that have led us to the present. We understand that we are caught up in a cosmogenesis and that we are creating and developing a new mode of religious consciousness. We do not lose or abandon earlier forms of consciousness. They are integrated by the 'integral consciousness' (hence its name).

One problem is that this new way of understanding has neglected its own true meaning. It has taken it for granted that only quantitative measurements communicate things as they really are. But we have to understand there is another dimension, a qualitative dimension to the universe that has been there from the beginning. In the sixteenth and seventeenth centuries men like Descartes and Francis Bacon taught that the only spiritual reality was man's mind or spirit (*res integra*) and everything outside this was purely mechanical or materialistic (*res extensa*). But there is a spiritual dimension to the universe which our culture has long neglected to recognize.

Even from the earliest times there was consciousness as well as a physical dimension to the universe. Thomas Berry points out that because the universe has produced imagination, sensation, thought, and feeling, there is sufficient evidence that the universe has immense and wonderful powers beyond any quantitative measurement. In his talks and writings he also points out that in returning to the source we learn that the basic norms of human activities can be discovered from within this deep spiritual process that is the universe itself, the universe that springs from ultimate reality.

*

Today we are living in a strong cultural trance. Mostly we are unaware of this, but it has infected us deeply. John Main speaks of this sickness when he describes man as having unleashed powers he can no longer control and of having exploited his natural resources so wantonly that he is in danger of exhausting them by the time his grand-children have reached maturity. We are aware of the vast devastation that has been unleashed on the physical body of the earth. Each minute more than an acre of rain forest is destroyed. Here on Vancouver Island, we are becoming acutely aware that our forestry practices have been less than perfect.

On the earth species are dying at an hourly rate. We don't know for sure how many species exist; perhaps ten million of the larger species. If we count all of the microbial forms there may be as many as a hundred million species. By the end of this century we may have lost as many as twenty million species. And there is nothing so absolute as the disappearance of a species. It can never be recalled. Never again shall we see the passenger pigeon or the Carolina parakeet. They are gone for ever. Irreplaceable topsoil is being washed into the ocean along with tons and tons of pesticides throughout the world. The ozone layer has been damaged to such an extent that we face the threat of deadly global radiation. At this very moment, the world in which we live is at risk. These are our current 'social sins' in terms of cosmology. Science cannot offer any quick fix. And the relevance of most theology is challenged by what is occurring.

All this is only a very small fraction of the ruin we are bringing upon ourselves, spiritually, socially, economically, and psychically. In the face of this crisis our governments and leaders, our churches and institutions continue to behave as if these very apparent signs of devastation are not the most crucial issues of our times and lives. We take it for granted that someone somewhere sometime will solve the problem for us.

It is exactly the same as with any personal illness: first

of all we have to admit that we are suffering. Since most of us prefer to remain in denial such an admission is difficult. It is essential to name the crisis that we live in and then learn to respond in an effective and healthy manner. This is perhaps our only hope, whether on a planetary or a personal level.

Once we have come to terms with our denial and anger about the state of our health, a greater challenge faces us: how can we deal with the problem? How do we recognize and then change the habits that have been responsible for our poor health, all of the alienation, and the deep pain? There is a place to begin. But first we have to realize what kind of a society we are living in and for which we bear the responsibility.

We are a dysfunctional society. For a lifetime, indeed for a millennium, we have been functioning out of a human–human, human–divine set of relationships, to the almost complete exclusion of the whole community we form with the earth and the universe. This is where our dysfunction arises which has caused the illness both of the earth and ourselves. Our ancestors assumed that we are separated from the rest of creation, that we are the sole species possessing intelligence, and understanding, consciousness, and a spiritual dimension. We have long assumed that we arrive at our destiny, our meaning and purpose, against a planetary and cosmic background that is purely physical, without a spiritual dimension. That is where our dysfunction lies.

We have ignored a spirituality of the earth. We need to discover this and embrace such a spirituality. The earth is no longer revelatory for us as it was before the end of the fourteenth century. We then had two bibles: the earth and Holy Scripture. They both were considered revelatory.

In the mid-fourteenth century Europe was decimated by the Black Death. Disease was not scientifically understood at the time. People thought they were being punished by God, that he was displeased with them. They began to consider the earth as evil. It no longer spoke of God. They wanted to escape out of the world. That there is a similar crisis in our time is self-evident. Not only must we become aware of this crisis and seek to alleviate it, but as part of our cure we must open ourselves to the stunning beauty of the Earth. What is needed globally today is a healing of the earth. But if we individually are not healed, if we do not undergo a transformation of body, soul, and spirit, healing can never take place. 'We shall not cease from exploration.' Our search is for something deeper than economic policies or political ideas. We seek a new way of life, a way of life that flows out of an awareness of the cosmic story and the holiness of the earth. We have to change the habits that have made us so very ill culturally. We have to discontinue the destructive, addictive, oppressive behaviour we have perpetrated on our planet.

*

We turn to the new story that is being told. This story is about a living universe. We have not understood that the

[38]

universe is alive. How do we get in touch with the notion of a living universe? We do this mostly through story. We come to see the universe anew. We come to see that the universe story is our story also.

There is something wonderful about telling a story. When someone tells his or her story, we are invited to enter and share that person's life. Also, it allows us to open ourselves to receive the beauty and message of the story. It is the same with the earth story. The story *is* being told. Every being is telling it as every being articulates itself.

The telling of this story should be the primary function of education. Indeed, we are not really educated if we do not know the story.

We need to see ourselves as that being in whom the universe reflects upon, activates, and celebrates itself in conscious self-awareness.

If we begin to experience ourselves in this manner, we see immediately how any degradation of the planet is adverse to our own well-being, physically, economically, and spiritually. If we allow such abuse of ourselves it indicates how little we love ourselves in the true and proper sense of 'self'. As Erich Fromm emphasized in his writings, it is necessary to love ourselves, to love the gift of being. To be human means to be in communion with the entire community of the planet. To be alienated from this community is to become destitute of what makes us truly human. And since we are bonded with every being in the universe, we cannot be saved without the entire community. When we damage this community we diminish our own existence.

*

I mentioned above how, twenty-five years ago, I did not receive permission from the diocesan council to attend an environmental conference because the environment was not considered of much importance to the church's thinking at that time. But recently when I requested permission and funding to attend a conference on Spirit and Earth in Seattle there was no hesitation in gaining such permission. We have moved a great distance in twenty-five years. The environment is now on the agenda of the churches.

At the conference Thomas Berry was one of the keynote speakers. Dr Brian Swimme also spoke eloquently, as did Jonna Macy, Sister McGillis and others. The Sierra Club had just published Fr Berry's *Dream of the Earth*. His writings had for long been circulated underground but are now not only being accepted by his own religious order, but also earning the respect of the church at large.

At the conference Thomas Berry and Brian Swimme stressed the importance of knowing the story, the New Cosmology. Our understanding of the origins of the universe and the planet which we call our home, they said, is growing. As this happens we are forced to rethink both our personal and our communal rôles and relationships within the unfolding story of creation. We need this new story (in reality, the old story) as a new way to see the cosmos. We need to enter into a human–earth relationship so that we can become a truly functional society.

Our traditional stories speak of a spatial mode of consciousness, in which time moves in a seasonal cycle of renewal. We have grown up with this story. Aristotle, for example, did not know whether he was closer to the Trojan Wars by going backward on the cycle of time or going forward. 'What is, has been. What has been, is.'

Thomas Berry stressed the fact that we are living in a different world, which can be described as a 'time developmental world', a cosmogenesis where we see an emerging universe going through a sequence of irreversible transformation episodes that bring us to where we are. This is the story that had to be told and retold and understood. Our single greatest need today is to understand ourselves as integral to this story. If we can understand the story, it will help us move into the future.

In the words of Thomas Berry, we must tell the 'new story' with a revised cosmological underpinning, because 'the Earth is mandating that the human community assume a responsibility never assigned to any previous generation'. We are being asked to learn an entirely new mode of conduct and discipline.

The transformation that we are to make is a fantastic one. We are at the terminal phase of the Cenozoic, a period of sixty-five million years which is coming to an end. We have to move into an emerging 'Ecozoic' era (a term coined by Thomas Berry). But how do we get there?

How do we go into the future? How do we 'know the place for the first time'?

As we begin to understand the story, there are certain things that, according to Thomas Berry, become clear and will enable us to move into the future, into the Ecozoic era. Some of these are as follows.

First, the universe is a community of subjects to be communed with and not objects to be exploited. Earlier we wrote that the basic norms of human activities can be discovered from the spiritual process that is the universe itself. Science tells us that there are three basic tendencies or laws of the universe: *differentiation*, *interiority*, and *communion*. These values that are basic to the unfolding of the universe.

From *differentiation* we discover the unique value of the individual being: no two drops of water, no two pine needles are the same. This reaches its zenith in the human being. Then when we turn to other beings of the natural world we are led to respect each being and to enter into communion with it. We come to learn respect for the individual, a greater regard for personal rights. Everything has rights. Trees have rights. Fish have rights. Instead of exploiting these individual rights we learn to respect them and enter into communion with each differentiated being in the universe.

Interiority, or the inner spontaneity or subjectivity of each being, means that each being has a capacity to articulate its own inner structure, to declare itself to the

[42]

entire universe, to be present to the whole universe. If we were sensitive enough we would detect this articulation, we would listen to every other being. We need to listen to the countless voices of earth and, indeed, the entire universe.

By *communion* we mean that each being bonds with every other reality in the universe. The whole universe feels the presence of each atom, since every atom affects every other atom, and all atoms affect the individual atom. It is really a cause of wonder when you realize that every atom in your body is in touch with and affected by the most distant star. We dance together in the great dance of energy. This law of the intimacy of things with one another is of immense importance for our survival. Thomas Berry says that it is the final expression of the curvature of space that holds all things together in a compassionate embrace that is the universe itself. Brian Swimme hints that love is constituted by that gravitational bonding of all beings, much more than by the strong or weak nuclear forces, or the electricomagnetic forces which, together with gravitational forces, form the basis of the universe. We back away from the thought of gravitational force being a bonding of love because we tend to think of these forces as purely material, forgetting that there has always been a spiritual dimension to the universe as well as a mechanistic force.

Second, the planet Earth is a one-time endowment. We don't get a second chance. There has always been the hope in the Judaeo-Christian tradition that we would enter into a millennial period of peace and justice and prosperity, a sort of heaven on earth. Or if things get too bad we can fly off to another planet. The fact remains that as far as we know, the earth is all we have. There are no new life forms being activated today from pre-life forms. The universe today, therefore, points to a new mode of religious consciousness. We are creating a fourth dimension of consciousness; or rather, we are being caught up in this new consciousness.

Third, the earth is primary; humans and all other beings are derivative. The earth is primary for our health. The first obligation of medicine is to bring about the health of the earth. You cannot have well beings on an unwell earth. Also, the earth is primary for our economy. What is the first obligation of economics? To bring about an integral gross earth product. We cannot have an increasing gross national product with a decreasing gross earth product. Such a situation would make no sense whatsoever.

Fourth, the Ecozoic era, which we might also call the age of the earth, is going to function very differently from the Cenozoic. The Cenozoic era now coming to an end did not consult us as to how many species of flowers and birds and insects we might desire or the nature of their song and beauty. All of this was given to us with no input on our part. All we can do is stand in awe and wonder at such magnificence, offer some appreciation, and perhaps sing a new song of praise. In the age of the earth, almost nothing is going to take place of any significance that will not in some way involve us and require an intervention and decision on our part. As Thomas Berry told us in Seattle,

> We cannot make a blade of grass. In the future
> there is liable not to be a blade of grass unless we
> accept it, protect it and foster it.

Then he pointed out, using the Exodus symbol, that the human community and the natural world will go into the future as a single sacred community or we will both perish in the desert.

*

There have been several outstanding events that have encouraged us to move into the future, into the age of the earth. In 1969, from outer space, we saw the pictures of the 'great blue marble' from Apollo I. Since then the idea has been growing that there is something extraordinarily holy about this habitat we share with all other forms of life. And then in 1992 one of the most important discoveries about the origin of the universe was announced. Suddenly it would seem science and religion have moved closer together. Scientists discovered wispy clouds or ripples of matter that indicate how matter that was uniformly spread out in the newborn universe may have started clumping together to produce stars.

Then the Earth Summit in Rio de Janeiro produced some magnificent statements. This conference of 179 member nations approved the Rio Declaration, a five-hundred-page programme to guide international action into the next century. There were also treaties dealing with global warming and biodiversity and the support of a permanent commission for sustainable development. On the other hand, the Earth Summit was not a complete success. It failed because the 'story of the universe' was not sufficiently acknowledged. It is the dream that drives the action, and we are still not sufficiently aware of the 'dream of the earth'. We have still not learned how to commune with nature, nor have we undergone the transformation of consciousness that is necessary if we are to see the unity of all beings and the non-dualistic nature of reality. And finally, and in my opinion the most important, we have not learned to pay attention. We have not yet learned, globally, to meditate.

> If we – you and I – are to further the evolution of mankind, and not just reap the benefit of past humanity's struggles, if we are to contribute to evolution and not merely siphon it off, if we are to help the overcoming of our self-alienation from the Spirit and not merely perpetuate it, then meditation – or a similar and truly contemplative practice – becomes an absolute ethical imperative, a new categorical imperative. If we do less than that our life then becomes, not so much a wicked affair, but rather a case of merely enjoying the level of consciousness which past heroes

achieved for us. We contribute nothing; we pass on our mediocrity.

– Ken Wilber, *Up From Eden*

*

Today it is clear that we stand at a turning point. It is the most critical turning point in the long history of the universe and of the earth. We are creating a new mode of religious consciousness which indeed is already palpable. But so far very few have entered into it. Until more of us do, our earth will continue to be threatened as we blindly close down our life support systems. To enter this new consciousness our ego, the 'I–Maker', has to die.

Our destiny is to bring about one of the greatest transitions in the story of the universe. Unless we enter into this transformation the next phase of the story will never come about. We are living in a transitional moment of the story. All such moments are sacrificial moments. We are called to make sacrifices. And the most difficult thing about this is that we must ask others to do the same. If the story can be told clearly, people will accept this need for sacrifice. Life teaches us that whatever is achieved has a price. We were given the beauty of the universe. We must make a response to it. We offer the gift of gratitude in return for the gift of the universe. We accept self-control as an aspect of gratitude. Ultimately we can only give back what we have been given.

We cannot just will the sacrifice. It has to flow from

love. That is where Ken Wilber is wise when he says that

> if we are to help the overcoming of our self-
> alienation from the Spirit and not merely perpet-
> uate it, then meditation, or a similar and truly
> contemplative practice – becomes an absolute
> ethical imperative, a new categorical imperative.

We need, then, to practise a truly contemplative form of
prayer, which will lead us away from our dualistic ap-
proach to reality. There are many forms of meditation, of
prayer, but in reality there is only one prayer: the prayer
that *is*, without beginning. It is the lifestream of Ultimate
Reality. It is the stream of love that flows between Jesus
and the Father, the Spirit of Love, the Holy Spirit. God is
not a static monad. God is interpersonal relationship,
interpersonal love. To the extent that we enter into that
stream we are carried beyond and outside of our narrow
selves, into the very life and love of the Godhead, far re-
moved from any dualism. As Christians, we open ourselves, by way of the mantra in meditation, to the
resurrected, glorified, infinitely transcendent human consciousness of Christ. Through his consciousness we enter
into that same relationship of love with the Father that the
Son experiences. It is our calling, our destiny, to become
this love in human form. Because the resurrected Christ is
also the cosmic Christ, in touch and in relationship with
every created being, we too enter (as we 'put on the mind
of Christ') into a non-dualistic relationship of love with

the entire human community and the community of the natural world. They become a single sacred non-dual community of love and sharing.

In our journey of exploration we move out of emptiness into the fullness of love. This is our calling. Herein lies our responsibility. The universe has poured into each of us those unique creative spontaneities that will carry us forward into the age of the earth, an age that even now is beginning to shine through as we create a new mode of religious consciousness. How necessary then it is to embrace those creative spontaneities which are unique to each unique being and placed within us to move us forward so that one day we will truly 'know the place for the first time'. We did not ask to be here. We were *called* to be here. Our gift of being is our most precious gift. As recipients of the gift we can but offer it back in gratitude.

*

There are many forms of prayer, of meditation, but only One Prayer. Up until, say, the end of the Renaissance, it was taken for granted that all were called to enter into this One Prayer. This call was a way of life. Prayer was like breathing. In the West we have had a long tradition of contemplative prayer which can be traced right back to apostolic times, leading forward then to the teaching of John Cassian in the fourth and fifth centuries. Cassian's teaching on the mantra in prayer became enshrined in the Rule of St Benedict in the sixth century, while in the East the Orthodox Christians adopted a similar prayer form that become known as the Jesus Prayer, memorably described in *The Way of a Pilgrim*. The tradition continued in the fourteenth century as found in *The Cloud of Unknowing*. I discovered the tradition of Christian Meditation in *The Letters of Dom Chapman* where he advises contemplative nuns who could no longer pray discursively to pray with a simple phrase repeated over and over again. In our own time John Main devoted himself to teaching this form of prayer. He had learned in the East to pay attention to God who dwells in the heart by preaching the same form of prayer that Cassian had discovered was used among the hermits in the deserts of the Middle East in the fourth and fifth centuries. In 1988, before travelling to India, I had the privilege of spending time with a community following John Main's teaching and learning from those who continued to teach it there this simple form of meditation with the mantra. Then in India I discovered that Bede Griffiths considered John Main the great teacher of our time. In recognition of this Fr Bede distributed the books of John Main and Laurence Freeman to all those visiting the ashram who had a thirst for contemplative prayer.

*

The practice and discipline (not 'technique') of John Main's teaching on what has come to be called 'Christian meditation' is very simple, but also very demanding. To meditate, sit down. Sit still and upright. Close your eyes lightly. Sit relaxed but alert. Silently, begin to say a single word. We recommend the prayer-phrase, *Maranatha*.

Recite it as four syllables of equal length. Listen to it as you say it, gently but continuously. Do not think or imagine anything – spiritual or otherwise. If thoughts and images come, these are distractions at the time of meditation, so keep returning to simply saying the word. Meditate each morning and evening for between twenty and thirty minutes. This is John Main's teaching on Christian meditation. His theology of prayer is summed up in his own words when he writes that there is really only one prayer:

> The central message of the New Testament is that there is really only one prayer and that is the prayer of Christ. It is a prayer that continues in our hearts day and night. It is the stream of love that flows constantly between Jesus and his Father. It is the Holy Spirit.
>
> It is the most important task of any fully human life to become as open as possible to this stream of love. We have to allow this prayer to become our prayer, to enter into the experience of being swept beyond ourselves into this wonderful prayer of Jesus – this great cosmic river of love.
>
> In order for us to do this we must learn a most demanding discipline that is a way of silence and stillness.
>
> It is as though we have to create a space within ourselves that will allow the consciousness of

the prayer of Jesus to envelop us in this powerful
mystery.

What does meditation have to do with the transformation of consciousness that will enable us to cease closing
down our life support systems? Ken Wilber clearly
teaches that if we are to contribute to evolution, then
meditation becomes an absolute ethical imperative. When
he speaks of evolution he is speaking of creating a new
mode of religious consciousness, a fourth dimensional
consciousness, of moving towards the Omega Point.

The form of meditation that John Main proposes is
non-objective meditation. As long as we continue to look
upon beings of the natural world as objects to be exploited, instead of subjects to be communed with, we will
continue our journey of destruction. Once we begin to
enter the world of non-objective meditation, we begin to
leave the world of dualism, the world of 'mine and yours'.

This rain forest is not my property, but God's creation.
It manifests God's hidden Being. In the words of John
Main,

> We find Christ in our hearts and then we find
> ourselves in him and, in him, in all creation.

To realize our unity with all beings, and so to leave the
world of duality is perhaps the most important step we
take towards halting the environmental destruction that is
taking place on the earth and in the universe. So we enter

into silence and stillness, exposing our human consciousness to the resurrected, glorified, infinitely transcendent human consciousness of Christ and, through him, we are carried to the Father.

Through Christian meditation we assist in the great transformation of human hearts and minds which leads the human community and the earth community into a single sacred community.

The World Community
for Christian Meditation

Meditation in the tradition of the early Christian monks and as John
Main passed it on has led to the formation of a world-wide community
of meditators in over ninety countries. Weekly groups meet in many
kinds of places and number over a thousand. An International
Directory is maintained at the Community's London International
Centre. A Guiding Board oversees the direction of the Community,
a quarterly newsletter, the annual John Main Seminar, the School for
Teachers, and the co-ordination of the Christian Meditation Centres
around the world.

Medio Media

Founded in 1991, Medio Media is the publishing arm of the World
Community for Christian Meditation. It is committed to the distribu-
tion of the works of John Main and many other writers in the field of
contemplative spirituality and interfaith dialogue. Medio Media
works in close association with the British publisher Arthur James.
For a catalogue of books, audios, and videos contact Medio Media Ltd
at the International Centre in London.

Christian Meditation Centres

International Centre

International Centre
The World Community for Christian Meditation
23 Kensington Square
London w8 5HN
Tel: 0171 937 4679
Fax: 0171 937 6790
e-mail: 106636.1512@compuserve.com

Australia

Christian Meditation Network
P.O. Box 6630
St Kilda Road
Melbourne, Vic. 3004
Tel: 03 989 4824
Fax: 03 525 4917

Christian Meditation Network
B.O. Box 323
Tuart Hill, WA 6060
Tel/Fax: 9 444 5810

Belgium

Christelijk Meditatie Centrum
Beiaardlaan 1
1850 Grimbergen
Tel: 02 269 5071

Brazil

Crista Meditacao Comunidade
CP 33266
CEP 22442-970
Rio de Janeiro RJ
Fax: 21 322 4171

Canada

Meditatio
P.O. Box 5523, Station NDG
Montreal, Quebec H4A 3P9
Tel: 514 766 0475
Fax: 514 937 8178

Centre de Méditation Chrétienne
Cap-Vie
367 Boulevard Ste-Rose
Tel: 514 625 0133

John Main Centre
470 Laurier Avenue, Apt 708
Ottawa, Ontario K1R 7W9
Tel: 613 236 9437
Fax: 613 236 2821

Christian Meditation Centre
10 Maple Street
Dartmouth, N. S. B2Y 2X3
Tel: 902 466 6691

India

Christian Meditation Centre
1/1429 Bilathikulam Road
Calicut
673006 Kerala
Tel: 495 60395

Ireland

Christian Meditation Centre
4 Eblana Avenue
Dun Laoghaire, Co. Dublin
Tel: 01 280 1505

Christian Meditation Centre
58 Meadow Grove
Blackrock, Cork
Tel: 021 357 249

Italy

Centro di Meditazione Cristiana
Abbazia di San Miniato al Monte
Via Delle Porte Sante 34
50125 Firenze
Tel/Fax: 055 2476302

New Zealand

Christian Meditation Centre
P.O. Box 35531
Auckland 1310

Philippines

> 5/f Chronicle Building Cor. Tektite Road
> Meralco Avenue / Pasig
> M. Manila
> Tel: 02 633 3364
> Fax: 02 631 3104

Singapore

> Christian Meditation Centre
> 9 Mayfield Avenue
> Singapore 438 023
> Tel: 65 348 6790

Thailand

> Christian Meditation Centre
> 51/1 Sedsiri Road
> Bangkok 10400
> Tel: 271 3295

United Kingdom

> Christian Meditation Centre
> 29 Campden Hill Road
> London w8 7DX
> Tel/Fax: 0171 912 1371

> Christian Meditation Centre
> 13 Langdale Road
> Sale, Cheshire M33 4EW
> Tel: 0161 976 2577

Christian Meditation Centre
Monastery of Christ the King
Bramley Road
London N14 4HE
Tel: 0181 449 6648
Fax: 0181 449 2338

Christian Meditation Centre
29 Mansion House Road
Glasgow
Scotland G41 3DN
Tel: 0141 649 4448

United States

John Main Institute
7315 Brookville Road
Chevy Chase, MD 20815
Tel: 301 652 8635

Christian Meditation Centre
1080 West Irving Park Road
Roselle, IL 60172
Tel/Fax: 630 351 2613

Christian Meditation Centre
322 East 94th Street No. 4B
New York, NY 10128
Tel: 212 831 5710

Christian Meditation Centre
2321 South Figueroa Way
Los Angeles, CA 90007-2501

Christian Meditation Centre
1619 Wight Street
Wall, NJ 07719
Tel: 908 681 6238
Fax: 908 280 5999

Christian Meditation Centre
2490 18th Avenue
Kingsburg, CA 93631
Tel: 209 897 3711

Hesed Community
3745 Elston Avenue
Oakland, CA 94602
Tel: 415 482 5573

Meditation on the Internet

WCCM.Archives
The WCCM, in collaboration with the Merton Research Institute
(Marshall University, USA), has archived a number of files: how to
meditate; biographical information on John Main, Laurence Freeman,
and others; International Newsletters; catalogues of books, audio-
tapes, and videotapes; the Rule of St Benedict and Benedictine
oblates; the International Calendar of events; John Main Seminars;
New Testament sources; and more. The Index of files and all individual files may be retrieved by anonymous FTP or the WWW using
the following URLs:

ftp://mbdu04.redc.marshall.edu/pub/merton/wccm/
http://www.marshall.edu/~stepp/vri/merton/wccm.html

The URLs for the Merton Archives are:

ftp://mbdu04.redc.marshall.edu/pub/merton/
http://www.marshall.edu/~stepp/vri/merton/merton.html

Merton-L is a forum for discourse on contemplative life. To subscribe, send e-mail to

listserv@wvnvm.wvnet.edu

containing the single line of text:

subscribe merton-l yourname

(substituting your real name for yourname, of course).

WCCM Forum
The WCCM.Forum is an outgrowth of the WCCM.Archives. Again, in collaboration with the Merton Research Institute, the expressed and sole purpose of the WCCM.Forum is to provide a place for substantive discussion on the daily practice of Christian Meditation as taught by John Main, the works of John Main and Laurence Freeman, and the work of the WCCM in general.

T6: WCCM, John Main, Laurence Freeman
In keeping with the expressed purpose of the WCCM.Forum as described above, posts about other types of meditation should not be posted to the T6 channel of Merton-L. (See the Merton-L faq for information about discussions on other channels.) Posts to T6 are moderated by the Merton-L owner(s) and are also monitored by T6 discussion leader, Gregory Ryan, who is the archivist of the WCCM

electronic files. Questions or comments of a personal nature or suggestions concerning T6 may be submitted to Greg via e-mail:

gjryan@aol.com.

To subscribe to T6
To join the channel one must be a present member of Merton-L or, if not, subscribe to it. To subscribe to Merton-L, send e-mail to

listserv@wvnvm.wvnet.edu

containing the following single line of text:

subscribe merton-l yourname

(substituting your real full name for yourname, of course). Anyone who has subscribed to Merton-L may join the WCCM channel by sending e-mail to

listserv@wvnvm.wvnet.edu

(from your subscription address) containing the following single line of text:

set merton-l topics: +T6

647 352 6646
Marsha